VISITS, PRISONS, FREEDOM AND A FUNNY LITTLE HILL

L. Peter Jones

ISBN 978-1-953223-64-7 (paperback)
ISBN 978-1-953223-63-0 (hardcover)
ISBN 978-1-953223-62-3 (digital)

Copyright © 2020 by L. Peter Jones

All rights reserved. No part of this publication may be reproduced, distributed, or transmitted in any form or by any means, including photocopying, recording, or other electronic or mechanical methods without the prior written permission of the publisher. For permission requests, solicit the publisher via the address below.

Rushmore Press LLC
1 800 460 9188
www.rushmorepress.com

Printed in the United States of America

Dedication

This little book is dedicated to:

GF, whose steadfast loyalty and love for
over 40 years boggles my mind.

My mother, who thought that anything
her children did, was 'great'. Bless.

John, an accidental editor,
And also to the lovely owners of 'Café Sixteen',
Sydney Street, Brighton, where I have spent many
Sunday morning hours working on this
damn book…blame them!

GOD'S VISIT

Not so very long ago, in a great, northern industrial town, a rumour got about that God was coming to visit.

At first, no one could believe it. People thought the rumour was either just silly gossip, or some sort of gimmick, dreamt up by advertisers – the brigade that is forever after your money or your time. So, most people ignored the whole thing, and got on quietly with their lives, while the godly nevertheless bowed their heads.

The weeks rolled by and, unaccountably, the rumour spread, gathering pace and credence until it came to the greedy ears of the very important people of this great northern industrial town, who, in turn, decided to take the rumour very seriously indeed! They argued that, as 'The Rumour' had gone viral, money was to be made, but only as long as *they* could control it! So, they set up committees and held meetings to discuss the details of what to do.

It was during a heated debate at one of these committee meetings, that the Mayor, a small but well-connected man with a great, big moustache and an imposing belly, announced that even if the rumour were some kind of cruel hoax, he, as Mayor, was going to go along with it, because, he fervently believed, it would be good for trade and great for tourism. To his inordinate surprise - and huge relief - everyone seemed of his opinion! And so a motion was passed to promote 'The Event' and allow 'The Visit,' even if it were not strictly speaking going to happen. And because 'The Visit' therefore became official, no one – especially not God - would catch any important person of this great northern industrial town napping.

Over the next few months, the town prepared. But as no one knew exactly when 'The Visit' was going to be, there were no deadlines to work to. 'The Works of God', or simply, 'The Works', which is what it became known as, just went on and on, without rest or respite.

Over the year, it seemed as if there was always something to do: palaces to be painted, frontages to be scrubbed and of course the main thoroughfares were thoroughly cleaned. There was, in fact, generally speaking, an upgrade for the few and stern words of austerity for the many. And the Mayor's resplendent coach dazzled in the sun.

Of course, 'The Works' cost a huge amount of money. And for some time, the politicians worried that it would be hard to pay all of the bills. But in no time at all, in another important committee meeting, they unanimously agreed on a new tax – The God tax - which helped immensely.

And then everyone waited: the rich, the poor, the priests and congregations, the politicians and the citizenry…and waited. The Mayor was heard to say, "Typical" under his breath at one particular meeting of misgivings.

So, a 'Crisis Committees was set up as the important people's credibility was at stake.

GOD'S VISIT

Despite the fear that this whole enterprise was rooted in nothing more than a rumour, it was agreed that 'golden eggs' and 'golden geese' should not be sacrificed for short-term doubt. There had been no visit - as yet - but business was booming.

Anyone who was anyone hoped and prayed that God – if He did turn up at all – would not forget all of their hard work! Some eyes looked at ledgers, while others only looked at the sky. And the godly prepared.

***

But, amazingly enough, God *had* turned up! It was just that only very few had recognised Him…to begin with. He had not come into the city riding a fiery chariot, nor surrounded by seraphim. There was no fanfare, no parade and no painted glory. He walked into the great Northern industrial town barefoot, worn with travel and care. He looked too thin for God, too much like a beggar to be the Almighty, *and* He came alone and unannounced.

As God walked the streets, He glimpsed the Mayor in his gilded coach as it processed past. He noticed crowded meeting rooms and conference halls, offices and memorial statues, palaces and pews, the prisons and the schools. He saw them all, and saw beneath and beyond. He saw the ruthless cleanliness of the High Street and the squalor of the unseen alleys

Wherever He walked, people stopped, people stared; whenever he spoke they listened and finally they recognised. He visited schools, and He visited hospitals and all the time there were the poor. And those He blessed.

He blessed all those who came to Him, all who stayed and all who heard with their hearts. And their spirits soared. And the children played around His feet, as they always had, knowing and not knowing, simply a mirror of Himself, a model, and a joy.

It was not long before this so-called beggar began to hit the headlines, as coincidentally, work on 'The Works' began to slacken. The very important people did know who He was or where He had come from. The very important people of this great industrial town were shocked. The very important people did not like the commotion, did not like the disruption and they insisted that 'the Show must go on!'

When the unseemly 'Beggar ' showed no sign of stopping his anti-social behaviour, the very important people became angry and had Him arrested for being a public nuisance. Their nice clean streets had to be ordered and under control before the Great Visit itself.

Meanwhile, in prison, God made many friends. Many of His fellow inmates were only there because they did not know Him, had never been shown who He was. Some, of course, had simply forgotten, and some were there because they had not been able to pay the 'God Tax'. God knew this; God knew everything. He smiled and showed them how to smile, too.

God smiled, they smiled; they smiled, God smiled.

And early, one wonderful morning, the warders smiled, too. They unlocked the doors and let the downtrodden free. They poured into the great northern industrial town, like a stream, which soon became a river and very soon a sea.

When schools were passed, they emptied, and as hospitals were reached, they were cleared. As more people heard, more people joined and more people listened. The Mayor was distraught! And as his infamous moustache twitched in frustration, his belly manoeuvred around his coffee and his desk. Yet another meeting had been called and the great and the good were all too busy to notice, too busy to listen, too busy to see and too busy to understand.

Eventually, this great northern industrial town ground to a halt as its people deserted its streets and only the very important people were left. Taxes went unpaid. And ruin stared at them in the face as they looked down into the abyss.

The important people passed emergency measures: things were sold, pawned or sent back…only slightly soiled.

The very important people felt hunger for the first time, fell sick for the first time. But they found no doctors, no nurses, no soup kitchens, no workers, and the churches fell silent while every candle blazed.

The Mayor took the decision on behalf of all the other important people, to seek out this Beggar, personally, to ask if *He* knew about 'The Visit', the only thing that could now save the town.

The great northern industrial town was on its knees.

The Beggar smiled.

He told the Mayor to gather up all of the important people and bring them to Him.

When this was done, the Beggar smiled again, and this time everyone smiled back. Because everyone had been found, everyone had been saved.

And then He led them away out of the town to where all the others were waiting for them.

And then there was great rejoicing.

I

We slowly scrape and draw the heavy metal bar across the hatch, to reveal a small, round peephole. One eye fixes to the cold, hard, over-painted greyness to see inside, while the other is squashed shut. Investigating like this, we think that discovering the other's secrets will be easy, and that what is on the other side of the door will be exposed completely. So, our nakedness focuses, adjusts, and lets the convoluted brain – in all of its lumpen majesty – take over and interpret what is framed before us.

Apparently, the harsh sound of the grating metal changed nothing.

There has been no reaction from the numbered soul, and he remains inert. He is like a slightly weathered statue commemorating something distant and something far off in time, but not quite human, a simulacrum only.

Yesterday, he was caught staring at a wall, the day before he was seen standing by the sink. Today, he is captured perched on the edge of his bed, doing nothing, saying nothing, revealing nothing, except, of course, that he is sly.

There is nothing to indicate here that he is even alive, save the deceptive calm, the measured breathing, and the imperceptible pulses spaced regularly around the body: timed, flowing, counting, sentenced.

We are wide-eyed in the act of lawful voyeurism and hooked. We want to know more. We want updates, upgrades. We want to study so that we can understand, so that we can avoid *his* pitfalls, *his* mistakes, and *his* blunders. It is easier to look at him than at ourselves. And even now the proviso is that there is a door between us, a locked door. We need protection: a kerchief at our nose, and a guard at our backs.

Compelling us to watch, an inner dare, the eye bonds to its Soap, is mesmerised and guided by our own desire for a happy ending, an excuse to chain ourselves here. For it is here, and in our reports, that we acknowledge that books have betrayed us, that our friends are strangers and that this gateway is the last chance saloon of solutions, the ultimate turn of the screw. We have become scientists, forgiving ourselves our sins in the name of research; we trespass because we have to, for we are the merciful and we tell ourselves, 'there is no other way.'

We watch, we learn, we supply details where there are none, fill in gaps where no gaps are, we create and imagine where we have no right and we soothe our own emptiness with the seeming fullness of others.

Ultimately, it is Fear that we seek to appease. We wish to cheat death and sidestep suffering. We hope to see what to avoid, and get clues on how to evade his suffering, his oblivion. So, we deepen our gaze, our guilt.

INSIDE

We see that he is covered in filth, maybe his own, or the cell's; none of it is ours. His clothes are torn, ragged, utterly spoiled; they are wrapped unevenly in a lifetime's worth of grime, his complicated skin, a tracery of compromise.

We also see that now nothing touches him, neither sight nor sound, neither heat nor cold; he has stopped like a clock. But he might stir, might be able to reveal his depths, our depths. Maybe. We stare. We hope.

There is a window in the cell, high up, small and stained. It is barred, though light does filter down, muted; it affects nothing, changes nothing because it seems to us that it is powerless, helpless, weak.

The man's eyes are closed. He can only feel the diffuse always-moted light on his exhausted eyelids, thin as paper. He looks like he is lost in the effort to be awake.

We reflect on him, but cannot conceive the inconceivable.

II

When Simon opens his eyes, he sees a great, green field peppered with flowers, an extravagance and an embroidery. It is a vision of a field, fantastic and full.

And the flowers he sees are gorgeous, every one, and they are beautiful as the sun is warm. There are pansies and violets, daisies and buttercups and more, a million more, and more still. They are all remarkable, all extraordinary even without the rosemary, even and because maybe they are so snagged and knotted, tangled and intertwined.

And, the perfect setting for them, the grasses in between, abundant and tall.

And high above, and spinning in clusters and crowds, birds swirl and swoop, in perfusion, and with mastery, their songs and screeches deafening. Everything is as it should be, the bliss of paradise, palpable.

Even the bees, those ever-popular pollinators, honey-makers, bumble along, like myths. And Simon is enchanted. He is captivated by this glorious display in front of him. He cannot pull away his gaze. He

INSIDE

looks, but Nature does not look back. He knows it pays him no heed. Still, he bathes in this joy and exuberance, standing as if for an eternity, at peace, enthralled.

He does not see the axe or scythe; he does not feel the dark wood, which surrounds his field, or its deep desire to cover the land again; he does not hear the breezy wish-washing sounds of the ancient trees as threats or cues. He prefers the green in frond and spore to their insistent age, rooted in the past.

And yet, deep inside, there is nag, and there is doubt. And it is bitter. And it is pain. But he cannot, nor wants yet to know; he is transfixed so completely by this beauty. This is his boundless happiness, his goal, his dream. Finally.

At his feet, a tiny distracting movement. Nosing for something small to eat, is a scabbed black mouse. It is sick with age and disease. It stumbles and stops. It looks up twitching, anxious not to become itself a meal.

Simon throws a crumb. But, for unfathomable reasons, before it can relish let alone taste his bounty, it dies, there and then, right in front of him. Sadness overwhelms and he is engulfed. Remembrance floods his brain and brawn and his slip-shod heart breaks: the flowers are all fighting; the birds all gorging on hapless prey and the forest looms in the chilling air.

IV

The man wakes up.
He stretches.
And then he sits on the floor.

Once again, he closes his eyes.
But now he knows.
He knows what chains are, what doors mean.
He unlocks, is unlocked.

He is aware
Of the goodness of a smile,
the rightness of light and love
and what freedom really is.

And then, without a flash or a thought, the man ... disappeared.

V

The eye does not know what it notices, but it recognises change. So, it – The Great Eye - hopes. And for a brief moment, its despair lessens - even at the light at the end of someone else's tunnel.

However, the man's fixed smile soon infuriates the Eye. It does not know why; cannot know why, which leads, inexorably, to more questions and then more; it guides more notes, creates more fury. There is no peace, at least today.

The Great Eye detaches, slams the hatch, and its world carries on regardless.

1

The hill – The Hill. The place where he played as a small child, the place where he went when he skived off school, the place where he could hate the world in perfect peace, his sanctuary and his only friend.

Before the Hill was sold to the old man, the boy was already an unreachable youth, unkempt and unloved. So, even before he met the old man, or knew anything about him, the boy already hated him. He hated the old man because he had taken from him the one thing no fence ever did. He hated the old man in the same way he hated all change, even those he craved.

2

Long, long ago, The Hill was colonised by a dense wilderness of woods, animals and the dazzling undergrowth of tangled plants and flowers, all of which flowed, unstoppable, over and across the great plain beneath it, linking it with the unimaginable vastness of the great primeval forests of the wider Old World.

When, inevitably, men found, on The Hill, a cave big enough to protect them, large enough to house and hide them, they massacred the indigenous bears and moved right in themselves. At first, they roasted some of the bear meat, using the plentiful dry wood that they gathered on The Hill itself, discarding what they did not want. Later, they roasted anything else they managed to scavenge by chopping down the living trees themselves.

It was not long before all the trees on The Hill had disappeared, and with them went the animals. And though the smaller plants did well for a time, they too slowly dwindled as the soil itself steadily slipped down The Hill, washed away by the rain onto the ever waiting land of the plain, where ploughing would start when men were good and ready.

THE HILL

When men left The Hill for the plains, they left no traces: they had made no strange drawings, images of bird, beast or prey, no lines of power, no outlined hands gave testament to their endeavours. Even the flames of their fires had not reached high enough to scorch the naked ceiling. Nor did they have the decency to leave any bones, theirs or their meals for our archaeologists to take away to their far-flung museums.

The Hill, poor neglected and denuded thing, remained unchanged, unloved and unobserved. It was never the navel of a cult; it was simply used and then forgotten, despite the more colourful years of civilisation: neither fort nor castle was ever considered; no folly in elegant spendthrift times; nor even a monument graced its banks, because The Hill was always too far from any interest, too mundane for worthwhile strategy, until, that is, came the old man.

3

No one knew whether the town started to grow up on the north side of The Hill for protection or from fear. But over the years, the town sprawled and spread until it resembled either a giant eye, with a huge, lifeless pupil, or a giant spoked wheel with a strange, rotten hub.

The boy's newest mother told him not to go up the Hill because only yobs went up there, and anyway, it was dangerous and unsafe.

No one needed a warning these days. The Hill wasn't cool. Even the kids had abandoned it for their electronics or the twenty-four hour shopping mall. But the boy still clung to The Hill. He still sat and stared and brooded, up there on The Hill. But when the old man appeared, that's when his world changed, when everything changed.

It was quite amazing that the sale of The Hill had caused such a stink as no one, apart from the boy, had even thought about it for years. Everyone just assumed that the Hill was theirs, an owned shared space that no one wanted or cared for, until that is, it was 'taken' away from them.

Interestingly, the concern, which rapidly turned to gossip, made people talk to their neighbours over the fence for the first time in years.

Some people even considered a protest, but when the local newspaper did an article explaining that The Hill - 'Our Hill' - had not been 'ours' for at least a hundred years, and had actually been owned by a manufacturing company, who had sold it, ridding themselves of a useless asset, the concern soon evaporated and no one gave it a second thought.

5

No one noticed a lone old man arrive. But everyone was affected, in some way, big or small, sooner or later. He was old and small and unremarkable save for his smile. However, inside his stout little body was a furnace of energy powering a mind as alert and attentive, as resolute and dogged as a sudden beam of light.

The boy could still not yet believe that his Hill had been denied him, could not fathom why someone would want to do this. But he found a way through the simple, unassuming fence, which had been erected too quickly to protect the new property, and no barrier at all to the boy. He climbed his Hill.

To his shock, the whole of the top of the Hill was gone; it had been completely removed and levelled. The foundations of a substantial house, or mansion even, with great geometric holes, were deep and clear and well defined.

How had he missed this? How could he have let this happen? The boy gritted his teeth and clenched his fists. This place had been his solace, his refuge, the one place where he and his mother had enjoyed together. Here, on this spot, they had had picnic, a place now emptied of meaning and soon to be enclosed in concrete.

"What 're you doin', Mum?" asked the child, his eyes, barely above the table. It was covered with food being wrapped or made, and his dirty little hands were gently smacked away.

"It's turned out nice, for a change. So we're going on a picnic!" she replied, with pride in her voice as well as a goal and a determination.

"Where're we goin' to have the bicnic?" asked the eyes swivelling up in astonishment and awe.

"On the hill," she replied. "Up there, right on top, where we can see the whole wide world!"

The boy instantly wanted to see the whole wide world almost as much as he wanted the jelly and cake, the butties and biscuits. And his little heart almost burst with happiness.

But it was all gone now. Bulldozed. And carelessly, thoughtlessly, swept away. And in the void that was left, the boy felt pain so acute, he needed something to hold on to. But there was nothing to hold on to.

He turned and fled. Down he went, down the hill, into brambles and thorns, down past old tracks newly torn apart, down the hill towards the insubstantial fence, which buckled under his blasting flood.

6

In the safety of his bedroom, there was no safety. The outside had penetrated like damp, and he was no longer in control. Darkness stole his mind as he drowned, sinking in his past.

The boy brooded till he schemed a plan: he would spy on the old man, spy on the works, tell everyone how bad it was and get things changed back to the way they were, back to normal.

And this sole, bleak hope roused him from his misery.

To climb the Hill, the boy cut across the fence, but only to be barred, once more. He could not find the old paths. In his absence, the old ways had been removed and *his* Hill had been refashioned and utterly reshaped. And now all roads led elsewhere. It was no longer his Hill. He had been erased.

The boy hid, shaking behind the great drop stone boulder, a random gift of ice that could not be moved, and slumped right down, his back against the cold, dead rock.

Head in his hands, the boy saw the ruthless plan, the unstoppable organisation. The old man had won. There was nothing he could do, but feel this bitterness and an eternity of hate.

8

The old man had seen the boy the first time he had visited the hill… and every subsequent visit, long before he had bought it, long before he had started his works. The boy and the old man were the hill's only visitors.

The old man could well imagine the boy's grief, his resentment and his hate. He had taken away the boy's space, his seat, his place in the world, and maybe even part of his identity. He could empathise with the boy's broken heart, even though he did not know who he was or his background. He made enquiries, discreetly.

The boy became part of his plan.

9

"Ask him to come to me," the old man told some workmen that he had hired. "Kindly, of course. Do not alarm him!" he added. The men knew the boy. Who didn't in this small community? They knew how to corner him!

Of course, the boy was sullen, obstinate and uncommunicative. But it was more than this - deeper and more complex. The boy was not able to speak, not just because did not want to, but because he was frozen in time, a voice paralyzed, so he could not explain his anger, could not vocalise his fear and could not confront the man who had remade his loss,

So the old man spoke for him.

"I can't imagine how you must be feeling," he said. "I came here, a total stranger, and tore your place apart, changing everything, destroying the very thing you love."

The old man paused.

"I am truly sorry for this," he said, but the boy blinked him away.

"But I came here - to your hill - with the best intentions," he said, and the boy's lips tightened.

"I came here to build a future."

The boy's forehead so wrinkled with contempt that he almost snarled.

"And I would like you to be part of that future."

Feeling nothing but contrariness, the boy looked away.

"Allow me explain what all this means," he said. "Let me show you my dream."

The old man led him to where his building was forming, big and round and dominating, erupting out of the wreck on top of the Hill.

"This will be a viewing platform," he explained with evident pride, his smile trying to coax and capture the boy's consent. "Contrary to popular belief, it's not a mansion. I would like the Hill to be a place that anyone and everyone can visit, so that they can enjoy the view. It'll be open – even in the rain. And it'll be for free…"

For he first time, the boy's armour was breached.

And thinking that the he had the boy's attention, the old man dared to drive on.

"From here," he said, smiling, "You will be able to see for miles and miles, like seeing the whole wide world…"

And with those words, the old man stopped, shocked. For he was witnessing the boy slowly crumple, like a controlled demolition, falling on his knees, as if praying, head down, eyes closed.

The old man said nothing, did nothing. He had never seen a reaction so strong, so genuine. He stood still and calm and patient. This was old pain still new.

After a while, the old man said softly, from his heart, "You see, I want to make this hill, your Hill, a beauty spot, a place where people, local people, can come and relax, restore their souls, if you will. I imagine people would like to have a picnic in a place like this…"

And then silence while, viscerally, piece by piece, the boy fell apart.

The old man could do nothing but be there, a witness and a charm. He stood stock still, throwing silent protection around this strange, young broken thing before him.

Feeling compelled to give the boy some hope, the old man continued:

"I want to restore this place, this funny little hill," he said, his voice tremulous, "I know you love this hill, *your Hill*, and it's important to you in ways I cannot fathom, but I am sure that you are the only one who can help me in this endeavour - you and me together. I have desecrated this place, in front of your eyes, but you and I can remake this place. Together, we can unlock the past to give the future a chance.

On the ground, the boy seemed cowed, bent, caged. But he was not.

"You don't have to decide now. Take your time to think about it. Let me know when you're ready."

Then the old man left the boy, taking his crew with him.

10

All night long, the boy stayed up there, a silent vigil, on top of the world.

Beneath the stars it was beautiful and cold, seeming still yet moving.

Eventually, the man unlocked, his mind danced and he saw the dawn and smiled.

11

And so a new partnership began.

They built foundations and they built walls.

They planned new paths together and prepared the beds for plants.

Together they sowed and together they nurtured.

Soon, there were blooms and birds, chirps and songs, shrubs and grubs and sap. To this place, animals flocked, or flew or crawled or dug.

And the eerie silence, which once had bound the Hill, was transformed. Sound returned. Meaning reappeared. And life came back.

"We should have a picnic," said the boy, smiling a secret smile. "With cake and sandwiches. You know, a real picnic. Not just lunch."

"What a wonderful idea," replied the old man, his heart bursting with happiness.

12

The old man died peacefully not long after the Hill was finished, but the young man had new plans of his own.

New avenues of trees sprang up in the town, and new parks, and, slowly but surely, the great green spaces spread, unfurling until they flowed unstoppable, chaining them to the unimaginable vastness of a brave new world.

And then he moved on…

13

One day, the old man came across a funny little hill…

CPSIA information can be obtained
at www.ICGtesting.com
Printed in the USA
LVHW030749301120
672995LV00006B/431